At the Zoo

by Spencer Brinker

Consultant:
Beth Gambro
Reading Specialist
Yorkville, Illinois

Contents

BEARPORT
PUBLISHING

New York, New York

At the Zoo

Where am I?
I am at the zoo!

What do I spy?

I spy a giraffe.

It is tall.

I spy an elephant.

It is gray.

I spy a bear.

It is wet.

I spy a flamingo.

It is pink.

I spy a snake.

It is long.
Hiss!

I spy children, too!

They are learning.

Key Words

bear

elephant

flamingo

giraffe

snake

Index

About the Author

Spencer Brinker lives and works in New York City. In such a big city, you can spy almost anything.